A PARTICLE

Love Poetry by

Cendrine Marrouat & David Ellis

Copyright © 2022 by Cendrine Marrouat and David Ellis

Book cover photo by Cendrine Marrouat

All rights reserved. No part of this book may be reproduced, stored in a retrieval system, or transmitted, in any form or by any means, without the prior written consent of the author.

Table of Contents

INTRODUCTION 1

CHAPTER 1 - MOMENTS OF BEAUTY 3

We 4

Tonight 6

Time Has Passed Us By 7

Sometimes 9

Similar Love 12

My Shelter Is You 15

Moments 18

Loving You 20

I Was Thinking of Us 22

Conversations 24

At Peace 26

A Poetic Moment 29

A Particle of You 31

Haiku 33

There Is a Love 34

Midnight, a Vardhaku 37

CHAPTER 2 - YEARNING, RETURNING 39

The Garden Beyond the Looking Glass 40

The Rivers Between Us 42

Two Different Voyages..43

Utterly Alive..44

The Tune She Hides Herself Behind 45

A Ballet in the Clouds 46

We Are Bound by Invisible Threads..............................47

Wait Till the Tide Takes Hold.......................................48

The Gift of Today..49

When Called to Heal..50

The Moment She Made Me See the Beauty in Everything 51

From the Last Sonata 52

Changed Into Wine 53

Pearls in the Midst of Night 54

Hear a Woman...55

Inside Silky Souls Laid Bare..56

ABOUT THE AUTHORS..57

INTRODUCTION

When I wrote my first poem in January 2005, I had no idea where this half hour of creativity would lead me. What started as a need to express myself and heal a depression that was then at its worst, became a lifelong passion that opened the door to endless possibilities.

If I had to do it all over again, I would not change a thing. Poetry has taught me to celebrate my own journey, love myself unconditionally, and share life's lessons in a way that I would not have found possible with any other form of expression.

To truly enjoy poetry, we must leave behind our preconceived notions of what the art form is supposed to be; and instead, let the words freely come and speak to us. The same goes for love, actually. The more we embrace it, the more we grow.

It may explain why so many poems talk about love.

I wrote the pieces in this collection over a period of sixteen years. Some are more positive than others. But overall, they have one thing in common.

The idea that there is no fulfilling existence without deep emotions.

Cendrine Marrouat

Winnipeg, Canada, July 9, 2022

If I am ever struggling to write, nothing stimulates my muse more than writing about something romantic. It encourages me to work with all of the senses and to connect with the reader that leaps off the page in deep, meaningful ways.

Love can mean so many things to different people but it is one of the fundamental emotions in this world that has the power to connect us all, with such a few words or actions.

I hope that you take comfort, solace and/or romantic inspiration from the pieces in this book. Cendrine & I have strived to provide you with a variety of poems that explore not only the nature of love and what it entails, but also universal themes that should resonate with you on some soulful level.

Thank you for reading and remember: There is love out there for everyone. You just need to keep your heart and mind open at all times.

David Ellis

Tunbridge Wells, July 20, 2022

CHAPTER 1 - MOMENTS OF BEAUTY

Cendrine Marrouat

We

A blade of grass,

A grain of sand,

We once were.

A tiny creature,

A large mountain,

We once were.

Part of the whole,

Sum of the parts,

We have been.

Phenomenal

Transcendence

Breathes in

And out of us,

Penning beauty

In every cell.

For we have been

Vessels of truth

Despite often

Edgy footsteps.

And the shadows

We bear confirm

Our kinship.

A blade of grass,

A grain of sand,

We once were.

Tonight

Blurry night. It was a blurry night.

Beautiful looks, harmony in full flight.

Arms brushing, what a delight!

Charming. It was very charming.

Smiling words, poetically alluring.

Hearts in thrall, what a craving!

Breathtaking. It was breathtaking.

Emotionally, it was more than inviting.

I would say that I felt it happening.

Now it's over. I know our souls had a lot to say.

We invented a world of unconscious play.

And that is what'll make us dream away!

Time Has Passed Us By

(Inspired by The Cinematic Orchestra's song *To Build a Home*)

Looking at you now,

As the green of leaves subsides,

I understand my purpose.

The light of your presence

Filters through the cracks of absence.

My soul knows what's right.

Time has passed us by

In this house others will not see.

Time has passed us by

But I will let you go.

My love, the dust will settle,

'Cause we are all made of stars,

And stars do not lie.

The ebb and flow of delight

Will be ours again someday.

Do not fear for me.

Time has passed us by

In this house others will not see.

Time has passed us by

But I will let you go.

Please close your eyes, now.

Sometimes

Sometimes, I miss you,

But not too much;

Just enough for memories;

Just enough to still care.

I don't believe in miracles.

I just think we weren't meant

For each other.

Sometimes, I love you,

But not as I used to.

We were immature

But full of sweet existence.

I don't believe in regrets.

I just think we weren't meant

To stay together.

I know there is a reason

For your love and treason.

Your ghost is far away now,

As well as our secret vow.

Sometimes, I think of you,

But not that much;

Just enough for memories;

Just enough to see the stars.

You don't need forgiveness,

And I don't have to apologize.

I was your alibi;

You were the love of my past.

I was your greatest alibi;

You were the love of my past.

Sometimes, I still miss you,

But not as I used to.

Sometimes, I still love you,

But not as I used to.

Sometimes, I still think of you,

But not as I used to.

Things may have changed,

But sometimes...

Similar Love

Hello, how are you?

Do I attract you?

Let's chat for a while;

I feel it's worthwhile

To know you better.

I like you, you're cute.

Let's dance a minute,

But, please, no fetters!

I don't do mornings,

I prefer evenings.

If you like that, then,

Let's kiss and amen!

Hello, how are you?

Do I attract you?

I've known you for years,

And as it appears,

I love you for real.

I wish I did know

How to let it go.

'Cause what I feel

Makes my heart shiver,

And my soul, quiver.

Please, try to love me.

I deserve our "we".

Hello, how are you?

Do I attract you?

We have shared life, love,

And the sky above

Has witnessed our fate.

You are my soul mate.

We are old and gray

But we walked the way

Few people dared choose.

There is naught to lose

With you in my life.

I feel blessed and rife.

I am a woman. You are a man.

But I heard of two women

Whose love for each other

Is deeper than the sky above.

And what about those men

We passed in the street on Monday?

Isn't happiness the only way?

Some choose one-night stands,

Others, life-long commitments.

There is no difference, because

Love will always play its part.

So let us never judge our brethren;

We might be caught red-handed

One of these days. Beware, for

Love is everywhere!

My Shelter Is You

Deep into the night,

He staggers along the shady street.

Bruised all over,

He can barely feel his body.

Darwinian obduracy

Allowed them to catch him dastardly.

Who will love him now?

And he bleeds and cries,

His footing uneven, unsteady.

But, people do not look.

They will not be bothered.

Like a malignant tumor,

They have excluded and lacerated him.

His tattered shirt bears the mark of

Society's loving caress and care;

His shabby-looking pants,

Now a dirty fusion of blue and red,

Are part of a throbbing past.

Who will love him now?

A few hours have gone by.

He cannot walk anymore.

Squatting down, his head in his hands,

He reflects on a time when

He had money in his pockets,

And a family to comfort him.

Where did they go on that August night?

He remembers the racket,

He can still hear the screams.

But, he will not look,

For fear he be bothered too much.

And the tears, they keep falling.

They fall until he can cry no more,

Until his skin loathes the wetness.

Suddenly, a sound, a word, a voice!

(A hand is reaching for you –

Grab it, do not let it go!)

Smiling eyes search for reasons.

A child again in these young arms.

And he falls asleep, solaced.

"I found you, Dad!" cries the son.

"I will never let you go again!"

Moments

I have had moments of love,

Moments of authenticity,

And moments of beauty.

Two souls entwined,

A fleeting bit of sensuality,

And smiles to die for.

Skins will not touch;

Eyes will not look;

Lips will not kiss.

Everything is within.

Energies explore the

Smooth flow of wonder.

How I crave those moments!

I have had moments with you.

One second was enough

To last me for eternity.

When shall we meet again?

I sure adore your soul.

Let us never make love.

I will show you heaven, instead!

Let us never touch or kiss.

I will write you poetry, instead!

I sure fancy your soul.

I sure miss your soul.

I have had moments of love,

Moments of authenticity,

And moments of beauty.

But, with you, one second

Was enough to last me for

More than eternity.

Loving You

Loving you is easy.

Your heart beats like

The midnight breeze,

Caressing the strings of my essence.

Loving you is easy.

Your smile tenderly

Invites reveries,

Exposing the chords of my mind.

Loving you is easy.

Your voice is like

Music to my inner ear,

And honey to my soul.

Loving you means completeness.

You answer the questions

Of my inner interactions.

You bless the seasons

Of my secret divinity.

God sent you to enlighten

The epiphany of my pen,

So that I can describe beauty

In words and thoughts,

And open the door to invisible realities.

Loving you makes me aware

Of my purpose in life.

Loving you brings me peace.

Loving you...

Loving you...

Is easy.

I Was Thinking of Us

This morning, I was thinking of us,

Just in time to watch the sun rise.

There was a part of me craving

The nearness of our devotion

And this amazing part of you

God showed me years ago.

Because it makes me smile

Whenever I feel blue.

Yes, this part of you

Keeps my heart full

And my eyes delighted

Every second of the day.

And when shadows claim their space,

Diluting the echoes of struggling light,

My heart knows how to find you.

Solace invites itself

In every speck of dust.

Bliss rests easy

In every chair we've sat.

My heart knows where to find you.

Conversations

I remember those conversations.

We were young then.

They had a flavour of insouciance.

Laughing away the pain,

We just enjoyed soft tides.

Atoms of joy and freedom

Intangibly surrounded us.

And then we became adults,

Pretending we were Peter Pans.

When all around us was changing,

We still laughed away the pain.

Our mise en scène was pretentious

To those who hate youth.

I remember their looks of envy.

And then, the dialogues

Continued, as though scared

To face the facts of life.

And then silence ensued.

I remember those conversations.

At Peace

He wakes up

And looks at her.

The beauty of his dreams,

The touching image of youth

He once breathed into perfection.

Without touching her skin,

He draws a map of joy

Across her face.

He is at peace

Because she is sleeping soundly.

The dust in the room

Has not once settled on her body.

A certain type of light

Now kisses her eyelids.

A slight tinge of a smile

Now appears on her lips.

She knows that she is loved.

She knows it so well

That invisible words can be heard

In this room where their bodies

First met, ten years ago.

She is the only one,

The only one who matters.

For what matters is infinity.

And she is a treasure-trove of it.

He stands up

And looks at her.

She is the mirror of his inner thoughts,

The passionate incarnation of his emotions.

And he knows that he is loved.

He knows it so well

That his mind shivers

At the thought of her kiss.

Outside, rain is falling.

And it is Sunday.

A Poetic Moment

A poetic moment between you and me,

Me and you. You... Me...

A split second of sensual discovery

When the heart whispers names,

Sings and flutters in the invisible,

Where space and silence meet

In a gracious dance of completeness.

Music, you will hear and embrace,

For God's tongue shall be uttered.

Hush and be still while I caress your mind

With pearls of wordless ecstasy.

Overflowing joyfulness of the senses—

Embryonic bursting of tenderness—

Manifestation of radiating fantasies—

Pulsating images of past visions—

When sky and horizon merge...

A poetic moment between you and me,

Me and You. You... Me...

A flitting instant of grand anticipation,

Of flowing enticing spiritual balance,

When nothing matters anymore,

When energy flows freely, happily.

Fingertips brushing against skin,

Skin drinking the beauty of silent intentions...

A poetic moment,

A dream of subtle creation,

When two hearts finally meet

And enjoy the solitude of Love.

You and Me,

Me and You.

You... Me...

A poetic moment.

A Particle of You

There is a particle of you

That I will love, always.

A speck of tenderness

Mixed with a grain of happiness

That I remember, always.

You are greater than you think.

That particle of you

Is a gift to the world.

It contains the essence

Of a bashful infant soul

That will soon grow.

Some may tease you,

But I never ever will.

Because, that particle of you

Is a speck of tenderness

Mixed with a grain of happiness.

And it is a gift to the world

That I will treasure until

It is time for us to part.

There is a particle of you

That I will love, always.

Haiku

the fireflies

coming from the east

words unspoken.

There Is a Love

There is a love

I know.

I know it more

Than anything else.

It has been high,

It has been low.

But mostly,

An alter ego.

It's been the kind of friend

I can call anytime—

Day or night,

Mad or sane,

Glad or inane.

This love I know,

Just is.

It has made sense

For decades!

It has been quiet,

A treasure trove,

And mostly,

A gift from above.

I feel it in the summer grass

And in the crisp winter air.

I hear it in the evening rain

And in silence's prayer.

I see it in your eyes

And in every sunrise.

There is a love

I know.

It has been high,

It has been low.

But mostly,

It has been mine

Ever since I learnt

To let go.

Midnight, a Vardhaku

Midnight,

the vast sea,

the nearness of vibrant constellations

floating at the edge of two worlds:

a wordless sonnet gathers between us.

The Vardhaku is a poetry form that I co-invented with linguist and short story writer Justin Smith in 2021, as an invitation to reflect on one's personal growth.

The Vardhaku is a portmanteau word consisting of the following elements:

- "vardha", a Sanskrit word meaning 'the act of increasing, giving increase or prosperity; augmenting; gladdening' or 'cutting, dividing' (Source: Monier-Williams Sanskrit-English Dictionary)

- "ku", as in 'haiku'

The Vardhaku is an expanding five-line poem divided into two parts: The first four lines describe a problem or situation, with the fifth line offering a positive / inspirational resolution. Title and punctuation are optional.

Using a combination of syllables and words, the Vardhaku mainly focuses on conciseness to deliver an impactful message to the reader. It must be composed in one of the following formats:

- 1, 3, 5, 7 words (lines 1–4) / 10 syllables (line 5)
- 1, 3, 5, 7 syllables (lines 1–4) / 10 words (line 5)
- 2, 4, 6, 8 words (lines 1–4) / 11 syllables (line 5)
- 2, 4, 6, 8 syllables (lines 1–4) / 11 words (line 5)

CHAPTER 2 - YEARNING, RETURNING

David Ellis

The Garden Beyond the Looking Glass

(Inspired by the Greek Fable *The Magician's Horse*)

Once upon a time

There, in a large forest

Beneath the stars at night

Stood a trace of human life

A living soul, with hunger and thirst

Lost in the flame of a fire, flickering

A glow spoke from it

Pure gold in a looking glass

Smouldering ruins, discovered, heard

Behind a mirror, there was nothing to lose

The sound of the earth, answered

"Fly once more and see the way!"

We must look back again behind us

When not able to advance, retrace steps

Hear the twinkling, the water, the fizz

Gather it, open a door of promise

Let anyone see and set out through beautiful paths

Everything loved from that moment, celebrated

Not to be left behind

You will find the sun glittering, in all directions

A rose in rebellion, disguised as a garden

Where the right of nothing but 'be themselves' is good enough

Be a hero for many and see a reward embroidered within

The Rivers Between Us

I owe so much to love

Relief, happiness, peace

The freedom love can give

I wait, patient, understand

A rendezvous is an eternity

Rivers between us

They live in lyrical space, genuine

They hold in their hands love's answer

Open

Two Different Voyages

Dreaming, were it not for promises

I had to mean them

You see in people properly loved, life

Of those dead and alive

A possibility without love

Gone on two different voyages

Drowning

Driven by determination

And hope

Utterly Alive

Our time is not the problem

It makes us feel like our own worst enemy

Better or worse, it is true

But we have to focus on what is still available

We have to hear music in the world

Understand variety

Know the pleasure of wine

Love and laughter are universal

Close our eyes

Savour the taste of us

We are utterly alive

We have the same emotional need

The Tune She Hides Herself Behind

In dandelion rain

The words she says, laughing

The sound of heartbeat

Draw near to her

The overlooked tune she hides behind

Walk, spellbound

Not even time approaches

Insist on happiness

Your arms, raised

This vision, you in love

Under trees, hushed

A Ballet in the Clouds

I must surely be warm

With thoughts green and gold

Soul filled up with only joy

Spirit swooping so high, against the blue of sky

Throbbing, trembling

Darkness, where careless hands destroy

Silver happiness

The wonderment of my heart

A mirrored pool, so deep

An instrument that can either sing or weep

We Are Bound by Invisible Threads

In the middle of love

Complete friendship

Each other, a mountain

Granular, we are huge, whole

Surely, this is fate discovered

In the night

You are the snow against the pane

Crystals, glistening

You hold my hand and I see beyond it

Wait Till the Tide Takes Hold

Time sometimes lied

Pain concealed, leaves a lonely ache

Darkness raw, rain on windows weeping

Remember to remain at ease

Wait till the tide takes even old, small memories

Loving lips left sweet relief

Kisses melt everything

The Gift of Today

Write me a library of love poetry

Waves crashing, let us caress forever

Savour moon, sea, constellations

Give into impossibility

Midnight fruit, a bouquet full of heat

Brush, blush, stroke, dream

Take rides, this carnival of life is short

Today is a gift, an open book full of promise

When Called to Heal

Oceans and skies, never ceasing

Stir spirits, a new yearning, returning

Tender remembrance of wild, sacred hope

Tears, the savage sound of human healing

The need of peace

Sense of benevolence

Tenderness, for passion deep from childhood

Shades of light, their sombre blaze will spread

Look up and dare to ask the truth

Save others to give life righteous paths for progress

The ultimate reward for the world rejoicing

The Moment She Made Me See the Beauty in Everything

Stroked silk, from her kiss

A glimpse of happiness

Forever, softly in everything

This moment with you, it's different

She sighed "I want you!"

Her eyes, bright

Lips remember, I didn't have to speak

You desperately wanted them

From the Last Sonata

Knowledge and desire

Truth, with consequences

Perception arises from any drama

Poetry moulding disparate acts

Because all share the same underlying music

Song, notes, beats, all are joined together

Follow and build from the last sonata

Lost in chaos, once again

Changed Into Wine

She spoke to me in champagne dreams

Fizzy exchanges, electric chaos

Golden giggling, tickling the sweetest spots

Disgorging sensory delights

Lasting, lingering, stars exploding

Wild, vintage desire

Intimate contact

Making everything else around us

Changed into wine

Pearls in the Midst of Night

Wild, endless dancing with her

Whose presence, overwhelmingly

Undulated into my heart

There we were

A sweet shifting of hair, eyes

Pearls in the midst of night

There we were

Gathering our time

Slowly, the fire reflected heavens, towering

Caught in sexual tension

Telling willing mouth to explode

Into unavoidable invitation

Hear a Woman

Illumination, waiting

They talk, whisper

Imagining something clear

Everyone else, is smaller

They hold hands

Turned on at midnight, again

Introduce her to wonders

When she sees light making love

Hear a woman

As she feels all

Inside Silky Souls Laid Bare

Endless embrace

Lipstick haze

Bare, silky souls

Threads magnified

Trace round bone, cheek

Coloured hues, bliss

Simmered intent, etched deep

Rivers rage inside

Filter noise, fight fear

Let life transcend shadows

Give tempered love, goodness, peace

ABOUT THE AUTHORS

Cendrine Marrouat is a poet, photographer, author, and creator of literary forms. She has released more than 40 books, including *Tree Reflections* (2022), *In Her Own Words: A Collection of Short Stories & Flashku* (2022), *After the Fires of Day: Haiku Inspired by Kahlil Gibran & Alphonse de Lamartine* (2021), *Songs in Our Paths: Haiku & Photography* (2020-2021), and *In the Silence of Words: A Three-Act Play* (2018).

Her work has appeared in many publications, including Synkroniciti Magazine, On Landscape, Real Creative Magazine, and eight cuts. She is the creator of the Sixku, Flashku, Sepigram, Vardhaku, and Reminigram.

Cendrine lives in Winnipeg, Canada

Website: https://creativeramblings.com

Email: cendrine@creativeramblings.com

Newsletter: https://creativeramblings.com/newsletter

Twitter: https://twitter.com/haiku_shack

Facebook: https://www.facebook.com/haikushack

YouTube: https://www.youtube.com/user/cendrinemarrouat

David Ellis is a poet, multi-genre writer/author and co-creator of literary forms, with a fondness for found poetry. He has released several poetry collections including *Life, Sex & Death* (which won an Inspirational Poetry Award), *Soul Music the Colour of Magic, Lemons, Vinegar & Unvarnished Truths, See A Dream Within* (based on the entire collected poetic works of Edgar Allan Poe), along with a Fifty Shades of Grey parody *50 Shapes of Cakes.*

Think of him like a thriller novel - fast paced, relentless and impossible to put down!

David lives in Tunbridge Wells, in the UK.

Website: https://toofulltowrite.com

Email: davidellisbusiness@gmail.com

Twitter: https://twitter.com/TooFullToWrite

Facebook: https://www.facebook.com/TooFullToWrite

Cendrine and David are the founders of Auroras & Blossoms, a platform dedicated to positive and inspirational creativity. Its flagship publication, the PoArtMo Anthology has given a voice to artists ages 13 and over from around the world for the last three years.

Cendrine and David have co-authored many books together, including *Seizing the Bygone Light: A Tribute to Early Photography* (2021) and *Rhythm Flourishing: A Collection of Kindku and Sixku* (2020). They have also created several poetry forms: the Kindku, the Pareiku, and the Hemingku.

For more information about Auroras & Blossoms, visit https://abpositiveart.com.

CPSIA information can be obtained
at www.ICGtesting.com
Printed in the USA
LVHW080037090922
727900LV00014B/450